BIOGRAPHIES

CRISPUS ATTUCKS

by Ellen Labrecque

PEBBLE
a capstone imprint

Pebble Explore is published by Pebble, an imprint of Capstone.
1710 Roe Crest Drive
North Mankato, Minnesota 56003
www.capstonepub.com

Library of Congress Cataloging-in-Publication Data
Names: Labrecque, Ellen, author.
Title: Crispus Attucks / Ellen Labrecque.
Description: North Mankato, Minnesota : Pebble, an imprint of Capstone, [2021] | Series: Biographies | Includes bibliographical references and index. | Audience: Ages 6–8 | Audience: Grades 2–3 | Summary: "How much do you know about Crispus Attucks? Find out the facts you need to know about the first person killed in America's fight for independence. You'll learn about the early life, challenges, and major accomplishments of this important American"—Provided by publisher.
Identifiers: LCCN 2020030680 (print) | LCCN 2020030681 (ebook) | ISBN 9781977132048 (hardcover) | ISBN 9781977133069 (paperback) | ISBN 9781977154057 (ebook)
Subjects: LCSH: Attucks, Crispus, –1770—Juvenile literature. | African Americans—Biography—Juvenile literature. | Revolutionaries—Massachusetts—Boston—Biography—Juvenile literature.| Boston Massacre, 1770—Juvenile literature. | Fugitive slaves—Massachusetts—Biography—Juvenile literature.
Classification: LCC E185.97.A86 L33 2021 (print) | LCC E185.97.A86 (ebook) | DDC 973.3/113092 [B]—dc23
LC record available at https://lccn.loc.gov/2020030680
LC ebook record available at https://lccn.loc.gov/2020030681

Image Credits
Alamy: Science History Images, 5, 29; Getty Images: Archive Photos, cover, 1, Hulton Archive, 15, Stock Montage, 19; Granger: 7, 9; Library of Congress: 13, 22; Line of Battle Enterprise: 21, 25; The New York Public Library: 6, 8; North Wind Picture Archives: 10, 11, 17, 18, 23; Shutterstock: Olena Rodina (geometric background), cover, back cover, 2, 29; Wikimedia: Daderot, 27

Editorial Credits
Editor: Erika L. Shores; Designer: Elyse White; Media Researcher: Svetlana Zhurkin; Production Specialist: Spencer Rosio

All internet sites appearing in back matter were available and accurate when this book was sent to press.

Printed in the United States 6797

Table of Contents

Words in **bold** are in the glossary.

Who Was Crispus Attucks?

Crispus Attucks was the first **patriot** to die in the fight for American **independence**. He was brave. He was willing to fight for America to be free.

In the 1700s, America was made up of 13 **colonies** ruled by Great Britain. Many colonists believed their lives would be better if they ruled themselves.

Crispus was once an **enslaved** man. He was also a colonist. In 1770, a fight between British soldiers and colonists broke out. Crispus was shot. He died for his country.

Growing Up

Crispus was born around 1723. He was born near Natick, Massachusetts. This was about 10 miles (16 kilometers) from Boston. His dad, Prince, was from Africa. His mom, Nancy, was an American Indian. "Attucks" came from Nancy's language.

Thousands of Africans were enslaved and brought to work in the colonies.

Enslaved people had to work hard without any pay.

Prince and Nancy were enslaved. As their child, Crispus was too. Life was hard for enslaved people. They had to do what enslavers told them. They worked all day. They were treated poorly. They were not free to make their own decisions.

an enslaved person running away with a bundle of his things

In 1750, Crispus ran away to escape slavery. He was 27. This was a brave thing to do. If Crispus was caught, he could have been killed. A notice about Crispus appeared in a Boston newspaper. It said that he ran away from an enslaver. But Crispus was never captured.

An ad in a newspaper offered a reward for the return of Crispus.

RAN-away from his Maſter *William Brown* of *Framingham*, on the 30th of *Sept.* laſt, a Molatto Fellow, about 27 Years of Age, named *Criſpas*, 6 Feet two Inches high, ſhort curl'd Hair, his Knees nearer together than common; had on a light colour'd Bearſkin Coat, plain brown Fuſtian Jacket, or brown all-Wool one, new Buckſkin Breeches, blue Yarn Stockings, and a check'd woollen Shirt.

Whoever ſhall take up ſaid Run-away, and convey him to his aboveſaid Maſter, ſhall have *ten Pounds*, old Tenor Reward, and all neceſſary Charges paid. And all Maſters of Veſſels and others, are hereby caution'd againſt concealing or carrying off ſaid Servant on Penalty of the Law. *Boſton, October* 2. 1750.

TO be Let, a convenient Dwelling-Houſe ſuitable for a ſmall Family, ſcituate in ...-Street at the South-End. Inquire

After Slavery

It is not certain what Crispus did after he escaped. Nobody wrote down what his life was like. Historians or experts believe he became a sailor. People who had been enslaved could be caught if they worked on land. While at sea, they were harder to find.

Ship captains wanted strong young men to work for them.

Sailors boiled whale blubber on ships.

Historians also think Crispus worked on a whaling ship. He may have hunted whales. Oil from whale blubber was used to light lamps. Whaling was a hard job. If Crispus was on a whaling ship, he would have lived at sea for six weeks at a time.

Historians think when Crispus was on land, he fixed ships as a merchant seaman. He cleaned the ships too. Crispus might have also worked as a rope maker.

No matter what Crispus did, he had to be careful. He didn't want to get caught. He didn't want to become enslaved again. He wanted to stay a free man. Crispus didn't use his real name. He told people he was called Michael Johnson.

Many ships sailed in and out of Boston's busy port.

Bravery

When Crispus lived in Boston, a lot of people were unhappy. Many colonists wanted to be free from British rule.

Great Britain used the colonists to make money. They made them pay taxes on things like tea and paper. Some colonists wanted to show the British king they were unhappy. They began to gather in big groups. They talked about ways they could change things.

Most colonists thought the tax on tea was unfair.

The king was afraid the colonists would break rules and start fights. The king sent soldiers to America to watch over the colonists. This made the colonists even madder.

On March 5, 1770, British soldiers stood in the streets of Boston. It was cold and snowy. The patriots did not like the soldiers. They did not want them in their city.

SHIP CHANDLER
DRUG STORE

Colonists often made fun of British soldiers.

The night was **tense**. A young boy and a soldier got into a fight. The soldier hit the boy with his gun. An angry crowd gathered around them. Church bells rang out. When the bells rang, more people poured into the streets. Crispus was eating supper. He ran into the streets too. Crispus and the crowd surrounded a group of British soldiers.

Patriots and British soldiers fought in the streets of Boston.

The crowd called the soldiers names. They called them "lobsters" because they wore red coats. They threw rocks, ice, and snowballs at them.

Crispus stepped to the front of the mob of people. He did not have a gun. He waved a big piece of wood. Crispus said, "Shoot if you dare!" The soldiers had been told not to use their guns. But they were scared too. Shots were fired. Two bullets struck Crispus. He died right away.

Four other colonists died because of the fight that night too. A funeral was held for the men. All the shops in Boston were closed for the day. Ten thousand people came to honor them.

A Boston newspaper ran a story about the funeral of the four men. A fifth man died of his wounds a few days later.

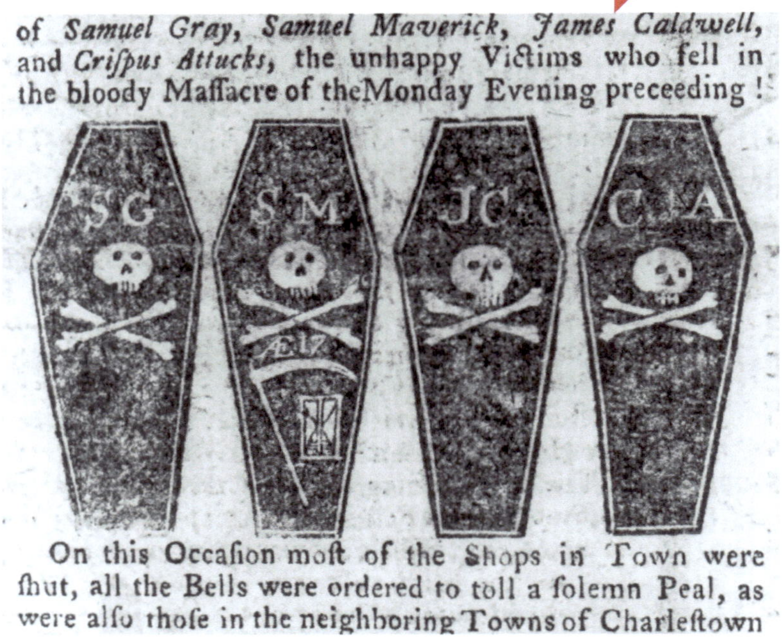

of *Samuel Gray*, *Samuel Maverick*, *James Caldwell*, and *Criſpus Attucks*, the unhappy Victims who fell in the bloody Maſſacre of the Monday Evening preceeding !

SG SM JC CA

On this Occaſion moſt of the Shops in Town were ſhut, all the Bells were ordered to toll a ſolemn Peal, as were alſo thoſe in the neighboring Towns of Charleſtown

Angry colonists demanded that the soldiers leave Boston.

The events that night would become known as the Boston **Massacre**. The soldiers were put on **trial** for shooting the five men. A **jury** found them not guilty of murder. Some of the soldiers were sent back to England.

Remembering Crispus

Crispus acted bravely. He was the first man to die in the struggle that became the **Revolutionary War**. He was a Black man. He had been enslaved. Yet, he still stood up for his country.

The war began five years after Crispus died. It started on April 19, 1775, when British soldiers fired shots on **minutemen** in Lexington, Massachusetts. The war ended on September 3, 1783. After colonists won the war, the colonies became the United States of America.

Battle of Lexington

More than 100 years after Crispus died, a statue, called the Boston Massacre **Monument**, was built in Boston. It honors the five men who died in the massacre. Crispus was the most famous of the men.

After the war, some Black American soldiers called themselves “Attucks Guards.” People wrote poems, songs, and stories about Crispus. Today, schools, teams, and parks are named after Crispus. He escaped slavery and died for America’s freedom. Crispus is remembered as a hero for all.

The base of the monument shows the scene of the Boston Massacre.

Important Dates

around 1723	Crispus Attucks is born near Natick, Massachusetts.
1750	Crispus escapes from slavery.
1770	The Boston Massacre happens on March 5. Crispus is shot twice by a British soldier. Crispus dies.
1775	The Revolutionary War begins on April 19.
1783	The Revolutionary War ends on September 3.
1858	Crispus Attucks Day is held on March 5 to remember the Boston Massacre.
1888	John Boyle O'Reilly writes the poem "Crispus Attucks."
1888	A Boston Massacre monument is displayed in Boston. It still stands today.

Fast Facts

Name:
Crispus Attucks

Role:
colonial patriot, killed in the Boston Massacre

Life dates:
around 1723 to March 5, 1770

Key accomplishments:
Crispus Attucks escaped slavery.
He became the first person to die in the fight for American independence.

Glossary

colony (KAH-luh-nee)—an area that has been settled by people from another country and is owned by that country

enslave (en-SLAYV)—to make someone lose their freedom

independence (in-di-PEN-duhns)—freedom from the control of others

jury (JUR-ee)—a group of people who listen to the facts of a case and decide the outcome

massacre (MA-sih-ker)—the killing of a large number of defenseless people

minutemen (MIN-it-men)—a group from the American colonies who were ready to fight with just a minute's notice

monument (MON-yuh-ment)—something built in memory of a person or event

patriot (PAY-tree-uht)—a person who supports their country

Revolutionary War (rev-uh-LOO-shuhn-air-ee WOR)—the American colonies' fight from 1775 to 1783 for freedom from Great Britain

tense (TENS)—a high-strung or nervous state

trial (TRAI-el)—the act of hearing a case in court to decide if a person broke a law

Read More

Siddons, Brian. *Crispus Attucks and African American Patriots of the American Revolution*. New York: PowerKids Press, 2015.

Taylor, Charlotte. *Crispus Attucks: A Hero of the American Revolution*. New York: Enslow Publishing, 2016.

Internet Sites

The Crispus Attucks Online Museum
www.crispusattucksmuseum.org/

Ducksters: American Revolution: African Americans
www.ducksters.com/history/american_revolution/african_americans_revolutionary_war.php

National Geographic Boston Massacre
ipod-ngsta.test.nationalgeographic.org/thisday/mar5/boston-massacre/

Index